eSPORTS

ESSENTIAL GUIDE

First published in Great Britain in 2020 by Dean,
an imprint of Egmont UK Limited,
2 Minster Court, 10th floor, London EC3R 7BB

www.egmont.co.uk

Written by Kevin Pettman
Edited by Craig Jelley
Designed by Smart Design Studio and Richie Hull
Gameplay images by Cloud King Creative
Cover design by Blacksheep Design
This book is an original creation by Egmont UK Limited.

© Egmont UK Limited 2020

ISBN 978 1 4052 9789 9

70863/001
Printed in Italy

ONLINE SAFETY FOR YOUNGER FANS

Spending time online is great fun! Here are a few simple rules to help younger fans stay safe and keep the internet a great place to spend time. For more advice and guidance, please see page 62.

- Never give out your real name – don't use it as your username.
- Never give out any of your personal details.
- Never tell anybody which school you go to or how old you are.
- Never tell anybody your password except a parent or a guardian.
- Be aware that you must be 13 or over to create an account on many sites. Always check the site policy and ask a parent or guardian for permission before registering.
- Always tell a parent or guardian if something is worrying you.

Stay safe online. Any website addresses listed in this book are correct at the time of going to print. However, Egmont is not responsible for content hosted by third parties. Please be aware that online content can be subject to change and websites can contain content that is unsuitable for children. We advise that all children are supervised when using the internet.

Egmont takes its responsibility to the planet and its inhabitants very seriously. We aim to use papers from well-managed forests run by responsible suppliers.

eSPORTS
ESSENTIAL GUIDE

WHAT'S INSIDE...

ENTER INTO ESPORTS!

Grab your controller, keyboard and headset – you're entering the epic eSports arena! From frantic team battle games to sick sports and mighty beat-'em-ups, there's an eSports scene and event for every gamer.

eSports are competitive computer games in which individuals or teams go head-to-head. This could be Fortnite, Overwatch, FIFA, Apex Legends, Rocket League and stacks more games. Contests can be played online over a season or at special events in huge stadiums, with thousands watching. The biggest players and teams become global gaming greats and win huge prizes!

The eSports world has exploded in recent years. It's estimated that over 400 million people watch eSports, with millions of viewers enjoying the action on platforms like YouTube and Twitch. This essential guide reveals all the top tournaments, teams and titles, plus loads of awesome eSports facts and stats. Game on, dudes!

LEAGUE OF LEGENDS

With 350 million viewers watching live League of Legends action on YouTube and Twitch each year, it's easy to see why it's one of the mightiest eSports! League of Legends was first released by Riot Games in 2009 and has bossed the Multiplayer Online Battle Arena (MOBA) scene ever since, helping make eSports a massive and exciting business.

LOWDOWN ON LOL

League of Legends (LoL) is a MOBA that pits two teams of Champions against each other across a three-laned map. There is a Twisted Treeline game mode for trios, but the 5v5 Summoner's Rift mode is the most popular. Teams begin on opposite sides of a map, aiming to reach the other side and destroy the enemy's Nexus tower. The Nexus is protected by turrets and auto minions that spawn and attack the opposing team.

CHOOSE YOUR CHAMP

Players have the choice of over 140 characters, called Champions. Each Champion has different skills and abilities that affect where they can best be utilised on the map. For example, some characters are great at causing mass damage at melee range, while others are good at hanging back and causing area-of-effect (AoE) damage from a distance.

SELECT A STRATEGY

Teams must work out a strategy that allows them to attack the other Nexus while also defending their own. There are three lanes on the Rift map leading to the opposing Nexus. Each member assumes a position in one of the lanes to try and push their offence forward and their opponents back. Some players, known as Junglers, roam between lanes to defeat neutral monsters, earn gold for upgrades and look for opportunities to surprise opponents.

LOL GLOSSARY

MOBAs can be particularly hard to understand, especially when you're communicating in-game. Here's a short cheat sheet with some common phrases you might hear.

- **BUFF** – A skill that increases a Champion's stats.
- **DEBUFF** – A skill that decreases a Champion's stats.
- **GANK** – To sneak up on a character in order to eliminate them.
- **JUNGLER** – A player who stays in the monster-filled jungle areas to collect gold.
- **LANE** – A path through the battle leading from one team's base to the other.
- **META** – The evolving playstyle and tactics of the game.
- **NERF** – When developers reduce the effect of a character or skill.
- **NUKER** – Champion that deals a lot of damage in a short space of time.
- **PUSH** – To advance down a lane by defeating minions and Champions.
- **TANK** – Durable characters that are usually the first to open battles.

LEAGUE OF LEGENDS COMPETITIONS

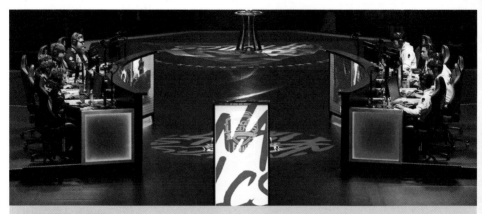

BATTLE TIME

There are 13 pro LoL circuits around the world. The five majors are the North American and the European Legend Championship Series, LoL Champions Korea, China's Pro League and Asia's League Master Series. These competitions, and other regional qualifiers, determine the teams that will compete in the biggest LoL tournament, the World Championships.

WORLD CHAMPIONSHIPS

At the 2018 League of Legends World Championships, Invictus Gaming (IG) took home the Summoner's Cup trophy after they whitewashed Fnatic 3-0 in the best-of-five final, setting a new record-low game time of 85 minutes. Invictus' heroic roster included LoL legends such as Duke, Rookie, TheShy and JackeyLove.

SKT1, Samsung and Invictus Gaming are the top prize-winning teams, each taking home over $3.7 million (£2.8 million) in prize money. South Korean teams tend to dominate the competitions, triumphing in the biggest events and pocketing more than twice the money of Chinese teams, though 2018 champs Invictus are based in China.

LEGENDARY LOL TEAMS

Most elite eSports outfits have a professional League of Legends team. It's a fast and frantic online game but also has huge cash tournament prizes. In the first nine years of eSports tournaments, over $65 million (£50.3 million) had been won by teams!

MAIN ATTRACTION

As well as being one of the biggest live eSports in stadia across the world, League of Legends is consistently top of the charts for online viewership too. Some tournaments can reach a peak of many millions of viewers on YouTube and Twitch.

PLAYER POWER

FAKER	DUKE	ROOKIE
TEAM: SKT1	**TEAM:** Invictus Gaming	**TEAM:** Invictus Gaming
COUNTRY: South Korea	**COUNTRY:** South Korea	**COUNTRY:** South Korea

Probably the most famous mid-laner in League of Legends, this super-skilful gamer picked up the World Championship trophy in 2013, 2015 and 2016.

Bossing the top lane, Duke's combat power saw him become the first player to seal the World Championship with two different teams – Invictus and SKT1.

Mid-laner Rookie used his mega MOBA skills to defeat Fnatic and take the crown for IG in 2018. He has won over $500,000 (£387,000) from LoL tournaments.

OVERWATCH

This hero shooter comes from legendary studio Blizzard, who are also responsible for the smash hits World of Warcraft and Hearthstone. With over 40 million players already and an enormous eSports stage, including the Overwatch League and World Cup, it's become one of the greatest first-person shooter games on the planet!

CHOOSE YOUR HERO

Before taking on the enemy, players choose a hero character from a roster of 30, including Junkrat, Reinhardt, Genji and Baptiste. Heroes are classed in Tank, Damage or Support roles and a team needs a perfect mix of skills to defeat their opponent.

ABILITIES

Each hero has different abilities that affect how you play. A Support character like Mercy can heal or boost allies, while a Damage hero like Torbjörn can set up turrets to attack enemies.

TOP TIP: Some weapons have a secondary fire method as well as the main one. Some weapons can lob projectiles, while others can freeze enemies.

PICK YOUR BATTLES

Overwatch is a 6v6 team strategy game with multiple game modes. Assault will have you battling it out to control or take capture points for instance, while Escort tasks the attacking team with shepherding a payload to an end point.

AROUND THE WORLD

The maps of Overwatch are spread across the world (and beyond!) and you'll rotate through a selection depending on the game mode. You could be battling through the cherry blossoms of Hanamura one minute, then defending your base on the Horizon Lunar Colony the next.

OVERWATCH COMPETITIONS

OVERWATCH WORLD CUP

The Overwatch World Cup is an epic affair that welcomes teams of international players from the best eSports outfits to join forces against other nations. The finals are staged at the annual BlizzCon event in California. In 2018, 24 countries competed for the cup.

FINAL FOUR

In the semi-finals, South Korea beat the UK and China saw off Canada to set up an all-Asian Grand Final. In a best-of-seven contest, South Korea swept past China 4-0 to clinch their third World Cup in a row. Canada pipped the UK to the bronze position by beating them in the play-off game.

WORLD CUP CHAMPS

The South Korean roster included Seong-Hyun 'Jjonak' Bang, the Support player from New York Excelsior team, who was voted Most Valuable Player (MVP). Players from Overwatch League teams London Spitfire, Los Angeles Valiant, Seoul Dynasty and Philadelphia Fusion made up the remainder of the talented Korean team.

OVERWATCH TEAM TRACKER

It's not just national teams that compete in Overwatch. Individuals and city-based teams from around the world also have their own competitions.

LEAGUE PLAY

The Overwatch Open Division is an official Blizzard competition where gamers from around the world aim to prove their battleground powers. The Trials and Contenders divisions are more challenging tiers for competitors, and above these still is the Overwatch League. Set up in 2017, with the first champs crowned in 2018, the Overwatch League was the first eSports contest to have city-based teams.

CITY GAMING

The Overwatch League has grown from its early days as a 12-team setup. There are now 20 teams from cities around the world, such as the Vancouver Titans, Boston Uprising, London Spitfire and San Francisco Shock. Teams contest around 280 matches in the regular season, aiming to get a slice of the eye-popping $5 million (£3.8 million) prize pool. After the regular season is finished, the eight best teams compete in the post-season play-offs for the chance to become league champions.

DID YOU KNOW? There's also an exciting annual Overwatch All-Stars game between All-Star players from the separate Atlantic and Pacific divisions!

INAUGURAL WINNERS

The two victors of the play-offs then contest the Grand Final. London Spitfire were the first champions, after they crushed Philadelphia Fusion in the 2018 final. They came out on top by a margin of 3-1 across the Dorado and Junkertown maps to complete a dominating display. The UK team collected a cool $1 million (£774,000) and Park 'Profit' Jun-young won the MVP award.

FORTNITE

Anyone who hasn't heard of Fortnite must have been living in an alien universe! Since 2018, it has become one of the most played video games of all time, with over 250 million registered players. Epic Games, the Fortnite developer, has huge plans to keep improving and updating the game with every new season. Find out all you need to know about the shoot-and-build phenomenon on the next few pages.

LET BATTLE ROYALE BEGIN!

Fortnite Battle Royale is an intense solo, duo or four-person squad game. One hundred players drop onto a huge island from the Battle Bus that floats across the sky, decide where to land and then begin to look for weapons, items and building materials with the aim of being the last player standing.

BUILD BATTLE

To become a master of Fortnite, you'll need to become a good builder - it's even more important than knowing how to wield the many weapons in the game. Building protective bases keeps your health and shield levels up and a tall tower is the perfect long-range sniping spot.

ESCAPE THE STORM

A storm rages on the edge of the map, closing in rapidly and forcing players out of their hiding places towards the fray. Every couple of minutes, the safe zone decreases and drives players towards the same location and into battle, where they fight it out for the best loot and weapons available.

LOOT PATROL

There's precious loot hidden all across the map, lying around the streets, buried in chests or stuffed in llama piñatas. The weapons and items you'll find range from common white loot to legendary golden varieties, which are way more powerful. Keep an eye out for the golden glow of chests!

FORTNITE HINTS AND TIPS

To become an awesome Fortnite eSports player, follow these crucial hints and tips ...

1 GET INVOLVED

The Fortnite eSports scene isn't for the weak – play aggressively, be bold and make yourself known on the island. Test yourself against better players and you'll boost your skills in no time!

2 BUILDING UP

It can be tricky at first, but make sure you master how to build quickly and what the best building types are. You'll never claim a Victory Royale without laying down some sick structures!

3 MAP IT OUT

The Fortnite map is constantly changing and updating. Keep track of the cool new places to loot and where game-changing items, like epic vehicles, are located to stay ahead of your eSports enemy!

4 SOLO AND DUOS

eSports events are aimed at both solo and team play. Play Fortnite by yourself and with friends so that when it comes to tournament time, you'll be equally comfortable in both solo and squad combat situations.

5 WEAPON KNOWLEDGE

Every gun serves a purpose and you should know which ones are best for each situation. For example, you'll need to know that a shotgun is great for close-range duels and rifles work best from distance.

6 SILENT APPROACH

Sometimes it's best to hang back, stay low and not blast the enemy. Firing is loud and alerts nearby enemies to your location. Choose when to harvest materials too as that's a noisy job.

7 TACTICAL TIME

Should you ramp rush the enemy? Camp in a high tower? Enclose them in a circle with the rest of your squad? Decide tactics within your team and keep a constant flow of communication between teammates.

8 MEGA MEDS

Shield potions, chug jugs, campfires and meds keep your health and shield at max. Keep these items in your inventory and know when to use and share them with your eSports squad.

9 WATCH AND LEARN

Seeing elite eSports players take down the opposition provides so much insight. Watch tournaments on Twitch and YouTube to pick up some pro tips – even watching your games finish after you've been eliminated can be helpful.

10 GAME TIME!

Keep playing and practising, no matter how you do in each match. Even if you get taken out in the first five minutes of the match, get back on the Battle Bus and keep playing. The more you play, the more you'll notice an improvement.

FORTNITE WORLD CUP

In 2019, Epic Games announced a cash-crazy prize pool of $100 million (£76 million) for its first year of competitive eSports gaming! The biggest of their events was the Fortnite World Cup. The World Cup was only for solos and duos, but unlike in other eSports, there are no team spots or franchises so absolutely anyone could enter.

ONLINE QUALIFIERS

The qualifiers for the World Cup took the form of an Online Open, split into regional qualification groups, such as Europe and Asia. Players competed against their regional counterparts for a spot in the World Cup final in New York, choosing either the Solo or Duos tournament.

NEW YORK FINALS

The Arthur Ashe Stadium in New York hosted the World Cup Finals and welcomed more than 19,000 fans over the course of a late July weekend, as well as the finalists in the Solo, Duos and Creative tournaments. Those who couldn't make it to NYC watched online - there were up to 2.3 million viewers watching the tournament at its peak!

CREATIVE

As well as the competitive tournaments, there was a challenge for the more creatively-inclined Fortnite players. A team known as Fish Fam, led by FaZe Cizzorz, beat out 7 teams to claim the first title of the weekend.

DUOS

In the Duos tournament, Aqua and Nyhrox beat their rivals to top spot and landed the first ever Fortnite World Cup Duos trophy. The pair, hailing from Europe, shared a prize pot of $3 million!

SOLO CHAMP

The main event was the finals of the Solo tournament, a fiercely competitive battle that ended with 16-year-old Bugha being crowned champion. The American scored a total of 59 points to take the top spot - over 20 ahead of his nearest rival - and landed himself a cool $3 million. The three runners-up were also North American competitors, so it was a good showing from the US on home soil.

DOTA 2

Get ready for some crazy numbers: Defense of the Ancients 2 (DOTA 2), the massive MOBA from Valve, is the biggest eSports title in history with nearly $180 million (£138 million) awarded to prize winners in over 1000 tournaments. The International is the most significant tournament in competitive gaming. Fortnite and League of Legends are hot on its heels, but the DOTA phenomenon shows no signs of slowing!

ETERNAL BATTLE

DOTA 2 was released in 2013 after the success of the original, which was a mod for Blizzard's real-time strategy game, Warcraft III. Two 5-person teams, representing the factions of the Radiant and the Dire, head into battle to destroy the other team's key structure, known as the Ancient, while attempting to protect their own from harm.

HEROIC ROSTER

Gamers select a Hero to play as, from a choice of over 100. The heroes vary wildly in their stats and abilities and each one lends themselves to a unique playstyle. For instance, Sniper is great for pulling off killshots from a distance, while Pudge can hook enemies and pull them in to attack at close range.

PRO TIPS

'Last hitting' is when pro players deal the final blow to Heroes and creeps lurking in the jungle in order to collect the Gold drops. Make sure to time your attacks just right when you're battling enemies alongside your team-mates to reap your rewards.

The best players will have experience in different roles, like Support, Carry and Jungler, to work out what their strengths are in each position. For example, if you tend to grow in power as the game reaches its conclusion, you'll likely be a useful Carry player!

Get to grips with new Hero releases straight away. Grimstroke and Mars were announced in 2018 and 2019 and top-level gamers were quick to get control of them and their powers.

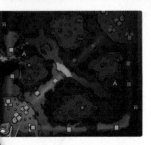

The mini map is a useful tool in DOTA. It's a small-scale map, showing the location of Heroes, creeps and buildings. The **scan** option highlights enemies – keep a watchful eye on it for any movements.

DOTA 2 THE INTERNATIONAL

Known simply as The International, this annual tournament is for hardcore DOTA teams only! It began in 2011 with the finals taking place in arenas in front of thousands of noisy fans over several action-packed days. Coverage is streamed via Twitch, attracting tens of millions of views and a large audience via US sports broadcaster ESPN.

ETERNAL BATTLE

The International has grown year on year, from just 40 players at the first finals in 2011, to 90 in 2019 with 18 pro teams reaching the finals. The prize pool jumped massively in 2014 when the DOTA devs, Valve, had the great idea to allow fans to contribute to the funds by purchasing exclusive Battle Passes. The increased cash had eSports teams scrambling for the crown!

YEAR	WINNERS	PRIZE
2011	Natus Vincere	$1 million
2012	Invictus Gaming	$1 million
2013	Alliance	$1.43 million
2014	Newbee	$5.03 million
2015	Evil Geniuses	$6.63 million
2016	Wings Gaming	$9.14 million
2017	Team Liquid	$10.8 million
2018	OG	$11.23 million

Split into an upper and lower bracket, China's PSG.LGD and Europe's OG won through to the best-of-five grand final. With the fab five of Topson, JerAx, ana, 7ckngMad and captain NOtail, OG captured games one, three and five as the contest went the full distance at the packed Rogers Arena in Vancouver, Canada. Topson's pick of the Zeus hero, in game five, was one of the major reasons why they saw off the challenge of a talented PSG.LGD team!

The International 2018 was the first time that winning teams from Dota Pro Circuit (DPC) qualifying events were welcomed to the main event, with successful teams from Major and Minor competitions winning through. In total 18 pro outfits reached the final phase, including Invictus Gaming, Fnatic, Vici Gaming, Team Liquid, Team Secret and Virtus.pro.

DID YOU KNOW?
eSports fans abbreviate The International to just 'T' plus the year of the event. So The International 2019 is 'T19'.

OG finally got their hands on the Aegis of Champions trophy, the most prized shield in the DOTA world. First presented in 2012 and taking more than 300 hours to craft, legend has it that it's made from dragon's skin and electroplated silver!

HEROES OF THE STORM

Blizzard is one of the slickest game developers and eSports leaders. When they created Heroes of the Storm (HotS), using characters from their awesome games WarCraft, StarCraft and Diablo, it was a dead cert to be a big gaming hit!

EYE OF THE STORM

Blizzard describes Heroes of the Storm as a 'hero brawler' and it utilises the same isometric perspective of many of the games they're most famous for, such as the Diablo series, which gives it an instantly familiar feel. As with most MOBAs, up to five players can form a team, picking a unique hero each.

HERO TODAY

Teams defend the Core by becoming a Hero, each of which has different powers and roles. HotS borrows some of their protagonists from other Blizzard games, like Genji, Lucio, Zarya from Overwatch and Blaze, Raynor and Sgt. Hammer from Starcraft.

BRAWLER

To keep the game feeling fresh, Blizzard included a mode called Heroes Brawl, which imposes different rules, twisted battlegrounds and limited characters to keep players on their toes.

PRIZE POOL

When the game was released in 2015 and started to become a major eSports event, Blizzard backed Heroes of the Storm with some serious prize pools. So far more than 50 events have had cash prizes of $100,000 (£75,000) or more.

TOP TEAMS

The HGC Global Championship Grand Finals was the most revered HotS competition. Staged by Blizzard in Anaheim, USA, eSports royalty like Gen.G, MVP Black and the Ballistix teams have all taken the title. In 2016, Blizzard even had a Fall and a Spring championship.

DreamHack, BlizzCon, Gold Club World Championship and Super League Heroes are other competitions where HotS teams have fought for success. At the end of 2018 Blizzard announced HGC 2018 was the final time it would stage the tournament, but the game lives on with passionate gamers desperate for domination with their favourite Heroes!

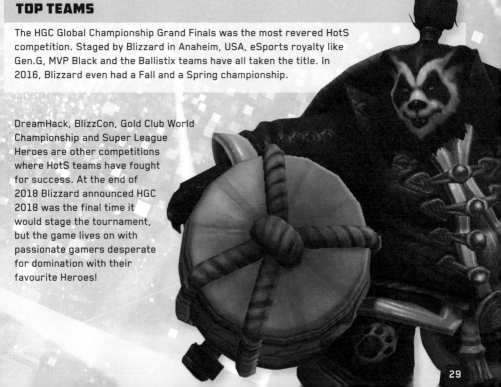

HEROES OF THE STORM TEAMS

Check out some of the hottest Esports teams and talent ever to take part in the Heroes of the Storm!

MVP BLACK / GEN.G

MVP Black scooped the Global Championships in 2017, before they became Gen.G and lifted it again in 2018! No other team has done the double like they have. Their all-South Korean roster of Ttsst, Reset, sake, Rich and KyoCha is one of the strongest the game has ever produced. Rich, KyoCha and sake have won more than $400,000 (£310,000) in Heroes of the Storm cash prizes.

BALLISTIX

In 2016, Ballistix's super squad of Jeongha, sCsC, Noblesse, Swoy and NachoJin marched off with the Storm Fall Championship and a mighty $300,000 (€232,000) prize. In the best-of-five final at BlizzCon, the Koreans comfortably beat Europe's Fnatic, with victory coming on the Towers of Doom battleground. Their damage dealing was just too hot! Ballistix also came third at the 2017 grand finals.

FNATIC

The perennial runners-up of Heroes of the Storm competitions are Fnatic. The team, made up of British and Swedish players, achieved second place at the 2016 and 2017 Global Championships. They might not have reached the pinnacle of this particular eSport, but they've still earned $930,000 (€721,000) from HotS events alone and the team, featuring Breez, Schwimpi and QuackNiix, will long be remembered by fans.

SUPER SMASH BROS.

Super Smash Bros. is a frantic brawler that pits up to four characters against each other in a side-facing map. It has been a party favourite for a generation thanks to its local multiplayer and shared screen, and made the step up to the eSports arena when Super Smash Bros. Melee was released on the Nintendo GameCube.

ACCLAIMED SERIES

Looking at the history of the groundbreaking Super Smash Bros. is like a guide to Nintendo consoles through the ages! The colossal battle game began in 1999 on the Nintendo 64. Since then gamers have also seen Super Smash Bros. Melee for the GameCube, Super Smash Bros. Brawl on Wii, a release for 3DS and Wii U in 2014 and Super Smash Bros. Ultimate for the Switch in 2018.

GUEST STARRING

As Nintendo has such a wealth of legendary games and characters to its name, it cleverly pulls these together in the Super Smash Bros. (SSB) series. It might seem crazy, but watching Mario, Yoshi, Donkey Kong, Pikachu, Peach, Luigi and Wario scrap it out is totally awesome! There are more than 70 characters to choose from, with more added all the time and others available through downloadable content.

PLATFORM BATTLE

SSB brawls are usually fought between single players, though they sometimes double up for two-versus-two tussles. The aim of the game is to knock, or 'smash', your enemy from a platform, rather than deplete a health bar. The pace is super-speedy and pro players can unleash multiple moves in the blink of an eye! Combining ground and air attacks with special moves is essential in this frantic fighting fest.

STREET SMART

There's lots of crossover between SSB. and the equally epic Street Fighter series, made by Capcom since the late 1980s. Most top eSports players compete in contests for both titles. Street Fighter V entered the scene in 2016 and welcomed back legendary characters such as Ryu and Chun-Li.

DID YOU KNOW?
Expert Street Fighter players like to test their skills playing in the original pixelated version, rather than the modern and crisp HD settings.

EVO

Super Smash Bros. and Street Fighter players will often compete at the Evolution Championship Series, sometimes known as just 'Evo'. It began in 2002, and became an annual contest where the best 'beat 'em up' gamers from around the world competed in front of thousands for global fame.

GROWING ROSTER

Several fighting titles are included at Evo and in 2018 there were eight crowns up for grabs, including championship titles for Tekken 7, Injustice 2 and Dragonball FighterZ. There are set to be even more titles up for grabs in the future - the biggest dedicated eSports fighting tournament in the world is getting bigger every year!

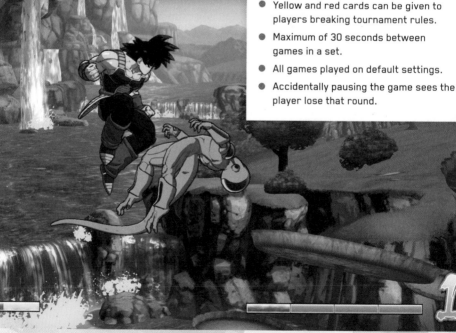

Evo Rules

- Players choose which side of the console to sit. If they can't decide, a game of 'rock, paper, scissors' determines it!
- Yellow and red cards can be given to players breaking tournament rules.
- Maximum of 30 seconds between games in a set.
- All games played on default settings.
- Accidentally pausing the game sees the player lose that round.

NEW CONTENDERS

Staged in the glamour of Las Vegas in 2018, the tournament welcomed over 11,000 participants across eight different competitions. All gamers are welcome – players book their place, arrive on the day and battle through the brackets. Famous champions can go head-to-head against plucky unknown gamers, which is ultra-cool for the fans.

SELECTED EVO 2018 CHAMPIONS

GAME	WINNER
Street Fighter V	Benjamin 'Problem X' Simon
Dragon Ball FighterZ	Dominic 'SonicFox' McLean
Super Smash Bros. Melee	William 'Leffen' Hjelte
Super Smash Bros. for Wii U	Bharat 'Lime' Chintapall
Guilty Gear Xrd Rev 2	Omito 'Omito' Hashimoto
Injustice 2	Curtis 'Rewind' McCall
BlazBlue Cross Tag Battle	Heiho

The Street Fighter V tournament alone had over 2000 players enter. The early rounds are best-of-three affairs, switching to best-of-five battles in the final stages. The UK's Ben 'Problem X' Simon crushed champ Hajime 'Tokido' Taniguchi in the final. However, he didn't manage to defend his crown at EVO 2019.

DID YOU KNOW? At Evo 2018, Team NRG won a special Super Smash Bros. exhibition match against Panda Global, Tempo Storm and Team Evo!

FIFA

When it comes to football simulators, there's one multi-million selling game that rules the pitch ... FIFA! Since the mid 1990s, the yearly release has grown and grown, captivating footy fans with its lifelike action and constantly updated teams. With over 30 leagues and more than 700 teams worldwide, it's no surprise that its eSports competitions are some of the slickest on the scene too!

LEGEND OF THE GAME

FIFA has been around for 30 years and was first released on the Sega Mega Drive and Super Nintendo systems. A new game appears every season with updated teams and player stats, and exciting new game modes, like Be A Pro and The Journey.

WHAT'S THE SCORE?

A huge part of the appeal to competitive players is just how precise the gameplay is. Each season, developers build on the tech, tricks and mechanics of the game. FIFA 19 boasted Active Touch Control, which improved ball skills and control. The addition of Timed Finishing boosted shooting accuracy, while enhanced team strategies were ushered in with the addition of the Dynamic Tactics function.

PREMIER PLAYERS

A new FIFA eSports championship kicked off in January 2019: the ePremier League. It was the official competition of England's Premier League and aimed to find the greatest FIFA 19 club player. Anyone aged 16 and over could register with one of the 20 Premier League football clubs and take part in an online competition to find the 16 best players on PlayStation 4 and on Xbox One. The 32 qualifiers attended a playoff, where the top player on each console went through to the London finals in March.

CHAMPIONS

At the finals in London, Liverpool's representative Donovan 'F2Tekkz' Hunt took on Manchester United's Kyle 'KyleLeese_' Leese in the grand final game, which was played across both the major consoles. F2Tekkz smashed his rival 6-2 over the two legs to walk off with the award. Liverpool may have slipped up in the real title race in 2019, but their eSports star managed to bring some success back to the city!

FIFA TOURNAMENTS

FIFA eWORLD CUP

The quest to be crowned the best FIFA player on the planet can only be decided through one tournament – the FIFA eWorld Cup! This is where the best of the best take to the virtual pitch for a series of intense matches. The event, which used to be called the FIFA Interactive World Cup, began in 2004 and nations such as Brazil, England, France, Spain and the Netherlands have lifted it.

WORLD BEATER

In its current format, competitors reach the grand finals through the Global Series qualification route. Millions of FIFA fans register and compete for Global Series points by winning games, with the top 60 reaching the playoffs. Then, the best 32 (16 from PlayStation and 16 on Xbox) enter games at the grand finals for the chance for a $250,000 (£194,000) prize. In 2018, Saudi Arabia's Mosaad Aldossary crushed Germany's Stefano Pinna 4-0 on aggregate to take the trophy home.

PAST WINNERS

The eWorld Cup has been running in some form or another for over a decade, and winners' trophies have travelled back to England, Brazil, Saudi Arabia and beyond. Here's a rundown of all the winners so far.

YEAR	eWORLD CUP WINNER	NATION
2004	Thiago Carrico de Azevedo	Brazil
2005	Chris Bullard	England
2006	Andries Smit	Netherlands
2008	Alfonso Ramos	Spain
2009	Bruce Grannec	France
2010	Nenad Stojkovic	Serbia
2011	Francisco Cruz	Portugal
2012	Alfonso Ramos	Spain
2013	Bruce Grannec	France
2014	August Rosenmeier	Denmark
2015	Abdulaziz Alshehri	Saudi Arabia
2016	Mohamad Al-Bacha	Denmark
2017	Spencer Ealing	England
2018	Mosaad Aldossary	Saudi Arabia

NUMBERS GAME

The stats around FIFA eSports tournaments are staggering! In 2018, over 20 million players took part in the Global Series qualifying events. In front of thousands of fans at The O2 Arena in London and with 29 million online views across all platforms, the grand final winner, Mosaad Aldossary, scooped his prize from a cash pool of $400,000 (£311,000). He also came second in 2019!

FIFA eNATIONS CUP

Another new FIFA tournament entered the fray in 2019: The FIFA eNations Cup. This competition is different to the eWorld Cup in that pairs of gamers work together, playing for their country in the hope of winning glory for their nation. In total, 20 countries were represented in the championship, including Argentina, China, France, England, Spain and Norway. It was the fab French duo of 'Maestro' and 'Daxe' that saw off Argentina in the final to secure the team a cheque for $40,000 (£31,000). The pair netted 1500 Global Series points each - these points count towards qualification for the eWorld Cup!

FIFA PRO TIPS

CONSOLE KING

As the finals of major tournaments are played across PlayStation and Xbox, don't just focus on mastering one console. Practise at a friend's house if they have a different console to you.

TACTICS TIME

Like in real games, playing with a tactic and strong discipline is the key. If you're protecting a lead in a game or an aggregate score, there's no need to go for all-out attack and risk losing the tie.

TEAMWORK

Most FIFA events are for solo players, but some, like the exciting eNations Cup, needs you to work as a pair with a friend. Practise your team-play skills and ways you can support your partner.

STAY UPDATED

Each season, the latest version of FIFA is used in tournament play. You'll need to get familiar with the latest release very quickly to learn all the new tricks, features and team dynamics if you're to have any hope of winning.

DEADLINE DAY

Many FIFA tournaments require you to sign up online before a deadline. Check you're able to join first of all, as there may be restrictions on age and region of participation, and make sure you get your application in before it's too late.

PITCH PERFECT

Lots of pro FIFA players say it helps if you play real footy, or even just have regular kick-about games with your friends. The Netherlands' Bob 'Bob95' van Uden was a youth player with Ajax, which he says helps him keep calm under pressure in eSports matches!

CLUB DREAM

With lots of practice and dedication, maybe one day you'll be signed as a FIFA eSports player for your favourite team. The clubs in England's Premier League, Spain's La Liga and France's Ligue 1 all have opportunities for gamers to represent them at competitions!

STARCRAFT II

Another of Blizzard's groundbreaking real-time strategy games, StarCraft II is the 2010 follow-up to the genre-defining Starcraft, released in the 1990s. With over $30 million (€23.5 million) awarded across 5,300 tournaments, it's the fourth-most lucrative eSport around and has huge appeal in arenas and for viewers at home.

COMMAND MODE

Starcraft II is a real-time strategy game that involves commanding units of varying types in a conflict between three galactic clans. You'll use your units to collect vital minerals, build structures and bases, and use increasingly more powerful tech to lead your army to victory.

SCI-FI SET-UP

The top competitions are for solo players, but StarCraft II is also able to host thrilling 2v2, 3v3 and 4v4 team play matches. There are four modes and three clans to choose from as you battle to lead your troops against the enemy.

FEARLESS FACTIONS

The three races in StarCraft II are Terran, Zerg and Protoss. Terran's key features include tanks, battlecruisers and flying buildings, as you control army units like the Viking and Helion. Zerg focuses on swarms of fast-moving beasts that can attack from below ground and the Protoss feature ancient warriors with rechargeable shields. As well as the competitive modes, SC II also has Story and Co-Op modes.

WORLD CHAMPIONSHIP SERIES

The biggest official Blizzard tournament for StarCraft II is the World Championship Series. This is the ultimate crown for Starcraft players and it has been staged every year since 2012, usually at Blizzcon. It was one of the first major eSports events. The format has been tweaked over the years, but now there are 16 grand final spots open to players from the Korean, Global and Circuit series. It always produces breathtaking action.

DID YOU KNOW? Nearly 2,000 pro gamers have competed in SC II events during the last ten years.

STARCRAFT II WCS

WORLD DOMINATION

The South Koreans have been the superstars of SC II, dominating the pro series and scooping over $10 million (£7.8 million) in prize money since the dawn of the eSport. Competitors such as Cho 'Maru' Sung Choo, Lee 'INnoVation' Shin Hyung and Lee 'Rogue' Byung Ryul all have more than $650,000 (£509,000) in prize money to their names. In fact, between 2012 and 2017, every World Championship Series winner hailed from South Korea.

STARCRAFT AT BLIZZCON

The WCS Global Finals are usually held during the BlizzCon event in California. In 2018, 16 players qualified by racking up enough ranking points earlier in the season. Half of these came from Korean events, the Global StarCraft League and Super Tournament, with the other eight coming from the WCS Circuit that spans Europe, Asia and North America.

FINAL FIGHT

Going into WCS 2018, hopes were high that Korea's hold on the trophy would finally come to an end. After already landing four Circuit events in Leipzig, Austin, Valencia and Montreal, Finland's Joona 'Serral' Sotala was the SC II man of the moment and hot fave in the finals. Maru and Rogue were aiming to shoot him down, though!

MVP

In the final eight bracket, Serral and Rogue stormed through to the semis. Kim 'sOs' Yoo Jin swept past Maru and Kim 'Stats' Dae Yeob also reached the last four in style. It was Stats and Serral who contested the showpiece final and a cheque for $280,000 (£219,000). Threatening a clean sweep, Stats bravely battled back from 3-0 down to make it 3-2, before Serral took control to finish him off and pick up the trophy. His first world title also made him the first non-Korean to be crowned the best Starcraft player on the planet!

HALO

The Halo series can look complicated, with several games in the main franchise and a handful of spin-offs since 2001. But for any newbies to the series, just remember that it's one of the finest first-person shooters ever created, which makes it the perfect eSport! In single-player or team play, this arena battle centres on grabbing a gamut of weapons, controlling a map and conquering the enemy. Ready up, Spartan!

SOLDIER ON

The Halo developers, 343 Industries, describe Spartans as 'super-soldiers'. They come from the 26th century, have biological augmentations and are the ultimate combat crusaders. Spartans are created with equal strengths and it's down to the individual talents of competitors and their decisions in battle to separate the best from rest!

STORIED HISTORY

Popular Spartans throughout the Halo series include John-117 (Master Chief), Kelly-087, Linda-058, Fred-104 and Will-043. The Spartans have tech augments that boost their shields, which players need to blast through in competitive play before they can go for the kill.

PRIZE POOL

Over the last 15 years, Halo tournaments have totalled around $12 million (£9.45 million) in competitive match prize pools. Over 300 tournaments have been held in this time, and the benefactors include some legendary eSports teams, including Team Envy, Evil Geniuses and Splyce. However, the most successful Halo team is Counter Logic Gaming, also known as Optic and TOX!

TEAM EARNINGS	
Counter Logic Gaming	$1.19 million (£938,000)
Splyce	$851,000 (£671,000)
Optic Gaming	$780,000 (£614,000)
Team Envy	$556,000 (£438,000)
Team Allegiance	$535,000 (£422,000)
Team Liquid	$335,000 (£264,000)
Evil Geniuses	$322,000 (£253,000)

HALO WORLD CHAMPIONSHIP

CHAMPIONSHIP ROUND

The ultimate prize for Halo eSports squads is to capture the Halo World Championships (HWC). Beginning in 2016 with a tasty prize pool of $2.5 million (£1.97 million), Counter Logic Gaming (CLG) took the crown and a cheque for $1 million! Their foursome of Frosty, Lethul, Royal 2 and SnakeBite then competed under the banner of OpTic Gaming the following year, besting Team EnVyUs to become double world-beaters.

TEAM PLAY

Taking place in Seattle in 2018, the HWC welcomed 16 qualified teams to a three-day event. These spots are earned as part of the Halo Championship Series and regional matchups such as DreamHack and the HCS Invitational. The final 16 are drawn in four groups of four, with the two top teams in each making the final eight bracket. Orlando, London, Sydney and Mexico City have all hosted the Halo World Championships.

TITLE RETAINERS

In 2018, serial champs Frosty, Lethul, Royal 2 and SnakeBite were known as TOX Gaming and were targeting a record three wins in a row. But number one-ranked competitors, Splyce, were the hot team to watch at the tournament. Both TOX and Splyce topped their groups and were joined by Str8 Rippin, Renegades, Team Envy, Elevate, Team Infused and Reciprocity.

DID YOU KNOW?
Challengers competed in Halo 5 from the Halo World Championships 2018 onwards.

FINAL FURY

TOX and Splyce destroyed all competitors in their way as they marched to the 2018 grand final. Splyce's squad was packed with the talent of Anthony 'Shotzzy' Cuevas-Castro, Kevin 'Eco' Smith, Jonathan 'Renegade' Willette and Braedon 'StelluR' Boettcher. In the last contest, Splyce battered TOX Gaming 4-0 to grab the title in the most epic way in front of thousands. In 2019, TOX were once again runners-up in 2019's HCS Invitational.

ROCKET LEAGUE

If you like racing cars and you're a fan of football, then Rocket League is the perfect mash-up for you! It allows you to control cool acrobatic cars in a futuristic arena as you try to smash a huge ball into the opposition's goal. Use boosts to power your car into position and master ground and air tricks to flick and force the ball around. Defend, attack and go nuts for this fun-packed sports game!

CAR-RAZY COMPETITION!

Not long after Rocket League landed in 2015, eSports teams spotted the chance to take part in competitive games that would be totally different to any other title. Companies like Electronic Sports League (ESL) and Major League Gaming (MLG) began to promote online and arena events. In the first four years, nearly 300 tournaments took place and $4.8 million (£3.7 million) was dished out in prize funds.

CHAMPIONSHIP SERIES

The quickest way to pocket some mega money in Rocket League is through the Rocket League Championship Series (RLCS). These finals take place twice a year, with prize pools ranging from $200,000 (£157,000) to $500,000 (£394,000). Game developers Psyonix runs qualifying rounds in North America, Europe, Oceania and South America and the ten best players speed into the finals.

DID YOU KNOW?
Dignitas player Jos 'Violentpanda'
Van Meurs is Rocket League's top
earner with more than $200,000
(£157,000).

PERENNIAL CHALLENGERS

Household US eSports teams such as
NRG, Cloud9, Rogue, Splyce, Ghost
Gaming and Evil Geniuses are regularly
among the competitors in Rocket League
championships. Challenging them from
Europe are successful counterparts
Renault Sport Team Vitality, PSG eSports,
Dignitas and Mousesports.

FIERCE COMPETITION

In 2018, Dignitas took the chequered flag
in the year's first RLCS finals. Up against
Cloud9 a few months later, they had no
answer to the skills of Kyle 'Torment'
Storer, Mariano 'Squishy' Arruda and
Jesus 'Gimmick' Parra. Cloud9's sharp
shooting and daredevil driving delivered
Rocket League's ultimate reward!

F1

There have been hundreds of racing games over the last 30 years, from the epic Mario Kart to the hyper-realistic Gran Turismo. The one game that's enjoyed a super-fast ride through the eSports arena is the official F1 game. It's stuffed with in-game functions and choices and can be enjoyed on PlayStation, Xbox and PC.

POLE POSITION

The aim is simple – just as in the real F1 season, gamers take control of a car from any of the competing F1 teams and race on all circuits for points. The player who has accrued the most points at the end of the season takes 1st place on the podium and the championship trophy! Cars can be developed throughout the campaign and even classic Formula One rides from past champions, like Senna and Prost, can be picked.

WHEELY AMAZING!

In 2018, F1 eSports racing saw a new format speed onto the grid. Over 66,000 online racers competed in qualifiers, hoping to make the Pro Draft. From these 40 Pro Draft slots, the final candidates were selected and drivers finally won the chance to represent one of the F1 teams in the Pro Series Championship. For these lucky speedsters, it was just like being behind the wheel of a 200mph Ferrari!

2018 DRIVER POSITIONS

1	Brendon Leigh	Mercedes AMG Petronas eSports	216 points
2	Daniel Bereznay	Mercedes AMG Petronas eSports	166 points
3	Frederik Rasmussen	Scuderia Toro Rosso eSports	127 points
4	Salih Saltunic	Sauber F1 eSports	83 points
5	Marcel Kiefer	Hype Energy eForce India	65 points

CHEQUERED FLAG

In November 2018, reigning cham Brendon Leigh clinched his second F1 PSC title. Competing for the Mercedes AMG team, he secured the trophy with a race to spare, after attaining first place in the Texas, USA circuit. Mercedes easily won the team standings. They pocketed a massive 382 points to Toro Rosso's 210. Unfortunately, Leigh and McLaren lost their crowns to David Tonizza and Toro Rosso in 2019.

APEX LEGENDS

The biggest videogame smash of 2019 was definitely the new battle royale Apex Legends! It pulled in an eye-popping 50 million players in the first month of release. It offers enough twists and turns to stand firmly alongside Fortnite. It became a hit for spectators online and it's only a matter of time before the eSports tournaments follow.

LEGEND LOWDOWN

Unlike Fortnite, which can be played in solos or teams, Apex Legends is for squads of three only. At the start of the game, the selected Jumpmaster decides when your squad leaves the dropship to land on the map, called Kings Canyon. You land with zero weapons and armour and must search for loot. The higher the tier of the items you pick up, the better chance you'll have against the other trios. As in all battle royales, the ultimate aim is to be the last one standing.

CONSTANT UPDATES

New weapons are dropped in the game all the time, including the Havoc rifle, which caused carnage in the first few weeks of gameplay. Keep on top of all the updates, new firearms and developments because these skills and powers give you the edge in Kings Canyon!

PROXIMITY BATTLE

As you move around the map, the 'ring' shrinks in on you and forces squads closer and closer together. Get caught outside the ring and you'll take damage every second until you can return to the safe zone within the ring boundary.

SELECT A LEGEND

In season one, Apex Legends came with a roster of nine Legends that players could use to dominate Kings Canyon. All of them have equal powers, but some are better suited to your combat style and preferences.

CAUSTIC

Real name Alexander Nox, he's a master of toxic gases that snuff out the enemy!

LIFELINE

A combat medic who looks after the team, but can take care of brutal business too.

MIRAGE

AKA Elliott Witt, this soldier likes to have a laugh and perform a vanishing act!

OCTANE

His bionic legs give him the springboard for daredevil displays in Kings' Canyon.

PATHFINDER

He's a MRVN (Mobile Robotic Versatile eNtity) and perfect for scouting and surveying!

WRAITH

The smart street fighter, watch out for her Dimensional Rift ability.

BANGALORE

The last in a long bloodline of soldiers, Bangalore has great offensive potential.

BLOODHOUND

With his hunting and tracking powers, it's a tough mission to escape him!

GIBRALTAR

Described as a gentle giant, his gun shield is a real life-saver in the Apex arena.

CLASH ROYALE

Card games may seem like a strange space for eSports to operate in, but they are a big part of gaming culture. Clash Royale appeared in 2016 and has already welcomed over 100 million players! Made by Supercell, the developer of Clash of Clans, Clash Royale is a great mix of collectable card games and impressive mobile tech!

HOW TO PLAY

Clash Royale is playable on Apple and Android platforms. In eSports competition, teams usually operate in 1v1 battles with opponents aiming to take down enemy troops, towers and crowns. Spells give you extra powers and character cards include Princes, Giants and Knights. The Clash Royale Crown Championship has a prize pool of $400,000 (£321,000) and Supercell also has its own Clash Royale League, with teams from every corner of the planet.

HEARTHSTONE HEROES

Blizzard specialises in strategy and combat games, but another of their top titles takes a different approach. Hearthstone, a rival to Clash Royale that was originally called Hearthstone: Heroes of Warcraft, is a digital card-based game where solo players use heroes and special cards to defeat each other's team.

CHEQUERED FLAG

Hearthstone was developed in 2013 and the Hearthstone World Championships began a short while later in 2014. With a prize pool of $1 million (£778,000) and an impressive $250,000 (£194,000) handed to the winner, the game's sickest stars fought like warriors for the award. Teenager Casper 'Hunterace' Notto, a native of Norway, is seen as the most consistent player of all time. After years of missing out, he finally got his hands on the world title in 2019 after beating Torben 'Viper' Wahl from Germany.

MINECRAFT

It has been impossible to escape the sandbox storm around Minecraft since it first gripped the gaming world in 2011. Creators Mojang unleashed a very simple, but hugely enjoyable creation game that can keep players busy for hours on end! Although its eSports arena is small compared to others, it will always have a spot in competitive gaming.

BUILDING BLOCKS

DID YOU KNOW?
Over 176 million copies of Minecraft have been sold since it was released in beta over 10 years ago.

Minecraft has seen few changes to its game mechanics since the original edition. It has such a monstrous appeal because its basic idea of building scenes and structures while interacting with others online works so well. It's a million miles away from the frenzy of a Fortnite or FIFA eSport tournament but there's a dedicated following for build battles and competitive minigames.

PRIDE AT STAKE

The cash on offer in Minecraft events is modest compared to the money madness of LoL or DOTA. For example, the Minecraft Monday tournaments in 2019 dished out just $10,000 (£8,027). Luckily, young gamers get involved for the glory and trophies that come with capturing a Minecraft eSport title!

SUPER LEAGUE

One of the most popular competitions is the Super League City Champs series in the US. There are 16 city-based teams, from places like Miami, Dallas, Phoenix, LA and New York, joining up to play Minecraft team games on their devices in cinema. Across four game modes, the 5v5 match-ups award a point to the winner of each mode. Los Angeles Shockwaves are traditionally the strongest, but at the season four Grand Final it was the Las Vegas Wildcards who managed to come out on top!

LOGGING OFF

The world of eSports has exploded over the last decade. In the future, there's every chance it will be as big a draw as the Premier League or NFL. At the start of the 21st century, who would have thought that massive prize pools could be won for playing computer games, or that crowds of up to 40,000 would fill stadia to watch them?

Teams like NRG, Evil Geniuses, Team Liquid, Fnatic, Cloud9, Splyce and Gen.G are known and followed around the world. Millions watch their favourite players on Twitch, and YouTube. T-shirts, hats and gaming products are emblazoned with team logos and proudly worn by supporters. Seasonal transfers of players between teams is big news. As games like Fortnite, Apex Legends, FIFA and Overwatch grow, the eSports scene will expand even further as new games bring new excitement! So stay tuned and keep your eyes locked on eSports … it's going to be a sick adventure!

IMAGE CREDITS

SAFETY NOTES

YOUNGER FANS' GUIDE

Spending time online is great fun. These games might be your first experience of digital socialising, here are a few simple rules to help you stay safe and keep the internet an awesome place to spend time:

- Never give out your real name – don't use it as your username.
- Never give out any of your personal details.
- Never tell anybody which school you go to or how old you are.
- Never tell anybody your password, except a parent or guardian.
- Before registering for any account, ask a parent or guardian for permission.
- Take regular breaks, as well as playing with parents nearby, or in shared family rooms.
- Always tell a parent or guardian if something is worrying you.

PARENTS' GUIDE

ONLINE CHAT

In most games, there is live, unmoderated voice and on-screen text chat between users. You may be able to turn off one or both of these options by looking in the Settings or Options menu in each game:

SOUND

Sound is crucial in many video games, particularly in eSports games. Players will often wear headphones, meaning parents won't be able to hear what is being said by strangers. Set up your console or computer to have sound coming from the TV as well as the headset so you can hear what other players are saying to your child.

REPORTING PLAYERS

If you see or hear a player being abusive, many games allow you to report users or interactions. Again, this will be included in the Options or Settings in most instances, but there may also be buttons within chat windows or game menus where you can raise a case with community managers.

SCREEN TIME

Taking regular breaks is important. Set play sessions by using a timer. Some games can last more than an hour and if your child finishes playing in the middle of a round, they could leave their teammates a person short and lose any points they've earned. It is advisable to give an advanced warning for stopping play or clearly outlining a stopping point before play begins.

IN-GAME PURCHASES

Many games offer in-app purchases to enhance the game experience but they're not required to play the game. They also don't improve a player's performance. Consoles and PC game launchers offer ways to limit spending by setting up parental controls. Consult these before allowing your child to play any game in order to avoid any unpermitted spending on your account.

GUIDANCE PEGI RATINGS

Many games in this book have guidance ratings, which, in the UK, are governed by PEGI (Pan European Game Information). Parents should be aware of the recommended age set by their local advisory board and decide whether their children should play.

- **League of Legends** - PEGI 12
- **Overwatch** - PEGI 12
- **Fortnite** - PEGI 12
- **DOTA 2** - No rating; see League of Legends
- **Heroes of the Storm** - PEGI 12
- **Super Smash Bros. Ultimate** - PEGI 12
- **Street Fighter V** - PEGI 12
- **FIFA 20** - PEGI 3
- **Starcraft II** - PEGI 16
- **Halo 5** - PEGI 16
- **Rocket League** - PEGI 3
- **F1** - PEGI 3
- **Apex Legends** - PEGI 16
- **Clash Royale** - No rating
- **Hearthstone** - PEGI 7
- **Minecraft** - PEGI 7